RANSACK AND DANCE

POEMS

RANSACK AND DANCE

POEMS

CHRIS FORHAN

SILVER BIRCH PRESS
LOS ANGELES, CALIFORNIA

ISBN-13: 978-0615827285

ISBN-10: 0615827284

Published by Silver Birch Press

Cover: British Library Illuminated Manuscript (Royal MS 12 F XIII)

Contact: silver@silverbirchpress.com

Web: silverbirchpress.com

Mailing Address:
Silver Birch Press
P.O. Box 29458
Los Angeles, CA 90029

for Alessandra

a sip or a spoonful won't do

Contents

Wild Desire / 9

Such Love / 10

Meager Furtive Little Wedding / 11

No Vows / 12

Against Transcendence / 13

There's a Second Time for Everything / 14

A Teleology /15

Elementary School / 17

Late Resolution / 18

Joy / 19

After Slipping and Floundering Down the Ladder / 20

Nine Sentences about Her / 21

Afterthought / 22

Dream: Faith / 23

To That Which I Follow / 24

Signs / 25

Aubade / 26

She Came with Long Hair, She Came Bearing Drink / 27

Why Did the Kissing Start? / 28

The Big Thing / 29

Renunciation / 30

Love Poem / 31

Solo Act / 32

The Severing / 33

Acknowledgments / 35

About the Author / 37

Wild Desire

I blame the animals, little ransackers,
black-eyed screechers through our sweet rows of corn.
They feast on what they find.

O tribe of light I long to join

I am not a skunk, I am not filled with garbage.
I have not the unearned royal mien of the rabbit
nor do I seek to anoint with musk
every shrub in the vicinity.

For my brooding upon an unbrooding life
of requited wild desire, I blame the animals.

Of what do they sing all night,
if singing it is, blood on their teeth?
The cricket thumbs his stubborn lighter
for hours, clicking away in the dark.

I shall rise one day as a flame,
no swamp's in this heart.

A bird builds his home of what is here:
a clump of human hair, a snapped thread.

A dog, the scent of his death in the air, slips
from the porch and slouches to meet it,
as if he would slobber on the hand
of his master. I won't have that. I just won't.

Such Love

I row and row, river water rimpling
behind me, like bed sheets I've slipped from,
like someone's memory emptying itself of me.

Such riproar and mischief, such unluck
the moon has witnessed and gloats above,
such love gone stupid. The human in me

makes a song of this, and of the trees
passing blankly on both banks. I swig
a rich red liquor, I drink and sing,

the tempo slow as that of my rowing
and of the bottles, spent, rolling and clinking
on the boat bottom. Such aloneness. Such ghosts

in the tangled drag of backwash: those I left
or who left me, because I sang and sang
of love but failed to love enough.

They turn their eyes from me. They're fine.
It's not their reproachful voice I sing to drown
the sound of. It's someone else's.

Meager Furtive Little Wedding

The one gift—that crate of sweet seasonings
from the east—we stowed in the cellar
and never crowbarred open: that was a sign.
And the way the priest blessed us
by miming the slipping of slack nooses
around our necks. Mistakes were made.
But the project went unscuttled
through fall, through winter, she in one room,
I in another, each of us writing and writing
of some other love having stripped us dumb once.
The potted plant in the stairwell, I will say now,
gave me the creeps, coiling and coiling
into a farcical tangle of limbs
we should have lopped off half of
to keep it from toppling. Our promise
was timid, so spring undid us:
a ruckus of rain, buds bursting
into sloppy blossoms, flaunty
reds and purples surrounding the house,
punishing us with the scent
of all the changes they'd braved to get that way.

No Vows

Once a god shot his voltage into me.
Once I felt kinged, like a checker.

I held my hand in a flame that crackled
and bowed. I was living

in a world I took for this one,
a world in which I licked sugar

from a woman's fingers, and she
licked mine, and we guessed that meant

each other's touch was trustworthy.
Some holiness swept over us—

in our certainty, we fumbled love away.
No vows now. I would have no one

bound on my account. This world
is for the distant, dexterous, and dissembling

to whom all blessings come. I shall seek
them now, and their secrets,

seek my comfort at the altar
of their spireless church.

Against Transcendence

Beyondness exhausts me:
the false promise
of the sea, steady exaltation
of waves, the summoning—

sky exuberantly blue
as if you could swim in it.

I strode wide of myself once:
that wedding is dead.

I served as witness
to my soul's long yearned-for
worthless and lonely enthronement.

I force no ghost to show itself.

I turn from the waves, turn
from the hills
humiliating themselves
with a cheerful late
sheen of snow, turn

from those pale-gold flickerings—
abandoned chapel deep
in a wood lit
by a single candle—

that are her eyes.

There's a Second Time for Everything

In the sky's poured tar: stuck stars
and one blinking little miscalculation
yearning along—a plane full of humans.

Who'll answer for that? Who'll answer
for all this arriving, all this desire that dies
to get there, then revives. Why these same

wasted acres to cross, then cross again,
between the lengthening tendril and the rot
in the strawberry. Always some loss is appalling us

into knowledge, some god's hauling fire
to where we can't find it. Why not
give that a rest. Why not a wedding for once

without a rose, without a bride, a heart
past ardor—an empty seminary,
doors open to the hard dumb wind.

A Teleology

The purpose of hail is to make you feel
unloved, as you do now: stooped
beneath your umbrella, parenthetical—
white bullets bouncing around you,
panicky bits of idiocy.

Hail so palpable it startles you back
into a day decades ago, into another
suddenness of sleet you sprinted through,
pressing sodden arithmetic worksheets
to your chest. Such is the way

of memory: a fish glinting to the surface
then vanishing through the murk,
leaving a brief burning in the eyes and throat,
a sweet Keatsian ache. The purpose
of Keats is to make you happily
melancholy over the smutch

your life has become, like yellow residue
in a shot glass, the causeway's last
gray indicium of a squashed frog.
The purpose of frogs is to stay frogs
and not be princes, but to bring princes
to mind—as the purpose of a prince

is to commission his image in marble,
whose purpose is to go unchiseled
if possible so we can't see the god in it.
The purpose of God:
The purpose of blossoms: to be gone, forgotten,
or plucked, tucked into a book, so we might

pretend death is a sleep. The purpose
of sleep: assent—as a song, dropped
onto a spindle and spinning, assents
to be played on a jukebox, whose purpose

is to stir in you a mood about the past,
about a record you half-remember
and would play, if only the jukebox
were not empty and unplugged, a dumb
emblem of nostalgia. But the song
is nearer than you know. It's a part

of the world, of the weather, like this hail
you've escaped by stopping
beneath an awning—it's an old melody
you've loved so long unthinkingly
everyone but you hears you humming it.

Elementary School

I was good all week, got
a gold star for it, so great
was my cowardice.

No muck in me, Mom.
When the flood came, I'd be there
with bucket and sponge.

In the meantime I hunched
at my desk, practiced subtraction,
lunched on whole milk

and baloney. My attendance
was perfect. I was conspicuous
by my absence, was nearly

a Bellini cherub already:
cloud-borne, smug
chubby head and feathers.

Wind, while my pencil drew
oval after oval after oval, what
shenanigans were you up to?

Snow swirling earthward
past the flagpole, what party gown
had you fallen from?

What would I think now
had I thought then
to swallow a palmful of chalk dust,

guzzle gutter water, give
a quick lick to Debbie's neck,
been more imperfectly dead?

Late Resolution

The future wished me well, then turned the pistol
toward me. I wouldn't want to be a rabbit anymore,
a panic of plans exposed in the open meadow like that.

I wouldn't want to be the boy I was, dismayed
by a girl who wouldn't deign to invade his privacy.
Where are the snows of tomorrow, I sang.

And where is that song now, that thumb smudge
of feeling I couldn't wipe from my glasses?
It's over, that flimsy overlap of oaths

and gusts of attitude that blew me here,
where the notion of consummation remains,
though only as warning. I won't be the past's:

I've shooed that goose. Nor the future's: whether
I'm handsome at the gallows or not—no matter.
What matters is this squall that's kicked up

and ripped the dogwood blossoms down,
a scattering of white velvet gloves in the grass,
more words for which I am suddenly at a loss.

Joy

It seized me—never mind the circumstance: sudden
scent in the breeze like cinnamon, sun silvering
a roof as the unicycle parade began—it seized me

as sickness does, wholly, with no mercy,
all of my body obeisant to its law as though none of it
were mine, finally: not the joy or the body.

After Slipping and Floundering Down the Ladder

The premise of this whacked, gashed ankle
and the debacle of blood it's made of my sock
is that my self-improvement project requires it.

Not so. My plan is fixed: no blood, no working
the brake and accelerator with the left foot, the right
wrapped tight in a paint-spattered sweatshirt,

no offering my body up to an intern's idea
of skillful stitching. Contingencies allowed
for the pretty widow to kiss me—but not

to go missing for weeks afterward, leaving
only a sentence of her voice inviting me
to speak to her machine. It was this voice

I had on my mind when my mind
was not on the ladder my body was on,
my right foot solidly setting itself

on air—a blunder that had nothing to do
with my to-do list: the few trifling miscues
and cunning recoveries I'll make to effect

an eventual permanent state of elation.
Unstipulated is this stoplight I'm stuck at
and this ice delivery truck I'm idling behind,

my fists wringing the wheel, ankle seething,
tongue seething, because it touched her tongue once.
It's not as if I've become a man who could feel

his face go red and wet, then press it hard
into a pillow to make this vanish, all of it—
the burning in the limbs and the bafflement

about a woman whose prettiness and kiss
are provisions I allowed for, but whose behavior
is now inapplicable, is in error.

Nine Sentences About Her

In my dream I am telling her my dream and she doesn't want
to hear about it.

I feel a little iffy, I say, unballasted, she says *Compared to what.*

We sprawl among the sheets, I kiss her hair, I whisper happy
birthday, she says *It's a lot of people's birthday.*

In the movie version of my life she plays herself and announces
she will appear in the movie version of my life but
otherwise forget it.

Play that song, she says, *the one that makes me think of you
thinking of me thinking of someone else.*

As she enters the room I see her first in the mirror or I see the
mirror first and she is in it.

I ask are you listening to me, she says, *Is it you who is speaking.*

She plays the man for once, I the woman, and Bogie-like she
grumbles *We had a laugh, kid, now buck up, you're
embarrassing yourself.*

In the poem I am writing about her I tell her I am writing a
poem about her and she says *If I were you, I would end
it here.*

Afterthought

The money I made lolling in soft grass
weighing words for the way the languid
willow dipped its leaves in the river:

squandered, all of it. When she left,
I felt unable to accuse her. I walked,
empty-pocketed, beneath a sky
that blushed crimson, like evidence of a crime

I'd yet to acknowledge. At the edge
of the wood, four crows screeched up
from the brush, settled on separate branches,
then flapped farther off from me

into the dark. I loved the letters of her name
first, then her trust and gentleness,
which means the love was suspect.

Dream: Faith

I'm crouched between orchard rows
picked clean, each scrap of green

unfastened, hauled off—
black clouds above the far hills:

a huddle of widows
mumbling—what?—*Love*

one thing in a rage if you dare
or nothing, no matter.

Face uplifted, I wait, it is
a bliss of rain coming, a tenderness.

To That Which I Follow

Where would you lead me now, blind ghost?
We have slipped past the guardhouse into the river.

I have sloughed the blue uniform, surrendered my anonymous
      body.
I have left the catastrophe of daylight stashed in a sack, turned
      my back on it.

Listen: I assent, I assent.

What immolation do you offer, what cure?
What lover in torn ribbons of wind, a dress of water?

Signs

Spin like this, the pinwheel, aflame in air,
whistled to me. *This way to the water*,

the half-drowned children sang, sopped,
hauled up blue. Crows screamed, laid siege

to the seeded field. *Careful*, the wind was careful
not to say, though I was born with a bubble

in my mouth: a harbinger, cardiac in nature.
I will not be glib about this. I gripped her fist

and kissed her. I was implicated. O
weighty world, lush, relentless: amid

your blossoming conflagrations
I understood I would not avert my heart.

Aubade

I lived in the liquor cabinet and my eyes got small,
eyes of a bird shot in flight. I loved then

wholly and only miracles, imprecations, spells
against she-who-left, spells against me—desperate

soupy concoctions: a skullful of brandy, a finger ring,
dirt from her final tire tracks in the driveway,

a shiny dime for luck. With a pocket mirror,
I drew down the moon to use later, when I'd undress

and wait at the graveyard gate, as spells of love instruct.
I was that alone, that drunk about it. You,

with gasoline to dowse all that, and the struck match,
you undressed me, dressed me down, swallowed

the sadness, slept on my chest, uncrippled it, you,
whose lost sock is in the sheets, you with blue hairpins.

She Came with Long Hair, She Came Bearing Drink

It gave me pause, that potion, but I sipped a bit, then chugged
    a jug of it.

O wasp, wasp at the window, she singled me out.

Cicada, I shrunk like you to a taut inch of shrill insistence.

I write of a woman who's real but goes unnamed here, appears
    as an acre of nectar, priestess in a wedding of tinder
    and flint.

And I am real: no longer a grumble, unbudgeable mood
    without meaning.

I drank and sank into myself again, sun-drunk, honey-drunk,
    too drunk to quit drinking, desiring only to be filled
    with drink, dumb-drunk, to drink and drown what I'd
    shrunk to when she found me.

Why Did the Kissing Start?

Because of leavings: silt-drift, silica
that falls and turns to rock in us.

Because we are foolish and will not last.

Because in the murk of dusk
she trilled to the bats in Italian.
Because she is pretty.

O my armada, in a minute
you were sunk, ocean closing
over the cannons and intricate rigging,
swift gift of absolution and forgetting.

Great blue herons, thruways—because
of them, because of the glut of comets
and eclipses amid which we have no choice.

Because we have blood in us and do not own it.

Because her imagination is a forest
with a fox in it, fur silver-tipped, glimpsed
and gone. Because we are unaffirmed.

Because we are death's pretty children
and task her patience. Because the heart

buries its losses again and again
till longing shocks it: bright sun
upon a white-washed necropolis.

The Big Thing

What goat goes roistering
through the bracken of my doubt?

What lantern lures me
from the cave I would have withered in?

The road is long and knotted, dear,
from the credulous dire country of boyhood

to your honest kiss. We pass the tool and die shop's
grind and click. You make a song of it.

I forsake my dead friend in a dream.
You ask how I have been forsaken.

Some depth charge has burst me into little fish
circling dizzily a bright spot in the water.

I might have been ash in the urn before this.
I might have refused to drop the knife

I'd been slashing my life with. I offer
what I have become for dismantling.

I confess I believe again in the Big Thing
and wish to be worthy of it.

Renunciation

Bundling my few things in a gum wrapper, strapping it
to a snail's back—I renounce that: the armor
of smallness, a pinched humility, a life as safe

as someone else's dreams. Calamity will come,
but it's not all sad sediment sinking in my blood
in the meantime, it's not just muck to give up on.

I renounce the creaky kneeler and funereal murmur
of the cramped confessional, the daily preparing
for death by being dead already. What I don't know

will hurt me. Until then, some predicaments are solved
by a new shirt. Until then, that's my pie. I reject
the snow globe, its caught water steadily

dwindling, disappearing into air. I will stay here.
I will not act doubtful of desire and call myself shy.
I will not be embarrassed by my own life.

Love Poem

I had to be batted balloon-like from the ceiling, then placed
in a small room: a cot, a tub, windows painted shut.

I was not a grown-up, I was air and failed potential.
Damp fuses were found in my pockets.

You were dropped on my tongue like a pill.
It was purely medicinal, to balance the blood.

But you stayed, and I struggled up from my bed, shed
my bandage, walked through the rain. It felt

unpurgatorial. Because of you, in the council chamber
I spoke loud and bold to support the safe playground petition,

because of you I saw Rome and Winnipeg, was robbed
but not shot, dreamed of your girlhood city

and woke accountably happy. Because of you
I live on the earth, sad and purposeful, like a stack

of fresh-cut lumber. Because of you my funeral music
will leave my friends' cheeks glittery with tears,

their hearts drunk with love for each other.

Solo Act

The moon, the moon put the screws to me
and shut me up. The phoebe trained me
to flutter from the cliff side,
a berry in my beak. No want in me
then, or human friend. I took
instruction from the dolphin:
nodded, grinned, skittered
backward across water.
A man can step from his life
as if from a bus, can settle
for thistle and bird song, wistful
safe elucidations of beauty.
Not for me to bleed
on the razor-wire; fox-like
I crept, would father
no daughter, hazard no son—O
son, I did not mean to lug
love to where you could not live.
Come out with your candle,
lean your ladder
against my branch, lift
a crumb in your cupped hand,
I'm hungry, hungry
enough, I think, at last,
to be defenseless against you.

The Severing

Any pistol I've touched was a toy. The hanging
of the tramp: that was two towns over—

I wasn't born then—and the boy roped
to a bumper, dragged down a back road,

bouncing: I heard about that on the radio.
One section of an animal can be severed

from the rest, it's swift. It's chance
I'm alive with my love and we dance

in the bedroom in socked feet, wriggling
to the hiccups of Buddy Holly, whose body

was silenced early, tossed to ice, and Marvin
Gaye (father, gun), *Oh mercy mercy*

me, he whisper-sings—we spin, leap, collapse
in the sheets, happily sleepy. For whatever

surgery that has cut us free in this way,
the instruments are tiny, and they gleam.

Acknowledgments

Grateful acknowledgment is made to the editors of the following journals in which these poems first appeared, often in alternate versions.

AGNI Online: "Why Did the Kissing Start?"

Antioch Review: "Elementary School"

Cerise Press: "Signs," "To That Which I Follow"

The Georgia Review: "Solo Act"

The Laurel Review: "Renunciation"

The Massachusetts Review: "Wild Desire"

Pleiades: "Love Poem"

Ploughshares: "The Big Thing"

Prairie Schooner: "Meager Furtive Little Wedding," "Such Love"

The Recorder: Journal of the American Irish Historical Society: "The Severing"

Red Mountain Review: "Joy"

West Branch Wired: "After Slipping and Floundering Down the Ladder," "Against Transcendence," "Late Resolution," "Nine Sentences about You," "A Teleology"

The title of "Meager Furtive Little Wedding" is taken from the screenplay of Alfred Hitchcock's *Marnie.*

I wish to thank the Corporation of Yaddo for the time and space in which to write these poems.

About the Author

Chris Forhan, born and raised in Seattle, Washington, is the author of three books of poetry: *Black Leapt In*, winner of the Barrow Street Press Poetry Prize; *The Actual Moon, The Actual Stars*, winner of the Morse Poetry Prize and a Washington State Book Award; and *Forgive Us Our Happiness*, winner of the Bakeless Prize. He is also the author of two chapbooks, *x* and *Crumbs of Bread*, and his poems have appeared in *Poetry, Paris Review, Ploughshares, New England Review, Parnassus*, and other magazines, as well as in *The Best American Poetry*. He has won a National Endowment for the Arts Fellowship and two Pushcart Prizes and has been a resident at Yaddo and a fellow at Bread Loaf. He lives with his wife, the poet Alessandra Lynch, and their two sons, Milo and Oliver, in Indianapolis, where he teaches at Butler University.